History

Shakespeare & Company

The Story of Lord Chamberlain's Men

By Paul Brody

BookCaps™ Study Guides

www.SwipeSpeare.com

Table of Contents

About HistoryCaps

HistoryCaps is an imprint of BookCaps™ Study Guides. With each book, a lesser known or sometimes forgotten life is recapped. We publish a wide array of topics (from baseball and music to literature and philosophy), so check our growing catalogue regularly (**www.bookcaps.com**) to see our newest books.

If you love Shakespeare, check out our free iOS, Android and Windows app: SwipeSpeare (**www.SwipeSpeare.com**)

Introduction

James Burbage founded the Lord Chamberlain's Men in 1594, during the reign of Queen Elizabeth I of England. The acting troupe was named after its wealthy benefactor, Baron Hunsdon, who later became Lord Chamberlain. During this exciting and tumultuous time in English history, this varied company of actors and writers lived and worked around London, plying their craft. Although it was a beneficial time to be in the arts, Elizabethan England did provide its own dangers and pitfalls. The wrong decision, or the wrong financial backer, could cost an actor his life. The actors played their parts on the stage, but they had just as many demanding roles to play in their lives. The competition was fierce and brutal, and often the troupes were used as political tools of the warring aristocracy. Playhouses, and acting troupes, rose and fell at the whim of the rich and powerful.

The troupe known as Lord Chamberlain's Men went through many members, and many incarnations, and during this time in history, established theatres were rare. The actors could just as easily find themselves working on an elaborate stage, funded by the wealthy, as they could find themselves performing from the front lawn of a seedy tavern. The very name of the troupe could change, depending on its financial backer, or the current political maneuvering of the troupe's owners. Security and stability were nearly unknown to acting troupes of this time, and they had to be ready to evolve with new circumstances at a moment's notice.

Although the tides of fortune of Elizabethan England ebbed and flowed with prosperity for acting troupes, and members often changed allegiance quickly, there were a few who remained constant with Lord Chamberlain's Men. These core members of the troupe were called sharers. As the name implies, they shared in both the duties and profits of the troupe. It is believed that there were always around eight of them at any given time in the troupe's history. They shared in the responsibilities of acting, supervising, and fund raising. And many times, they also shared in the physical duties of constructing the various theatres and acting venues in which they worked.

Serving as anchors during uncertain, chaotic times these individuals were the heart of the troupe. Of course, the most famous and arguably the most important sharer of Lord Chamberlain's Men was William Shakespeare himself. He was not a founding member, and it is thought that he arrived on the scene later. It is known, however, that he was their principal writer. And the marriage of his brilliant plays with some of the greatest actors of the time assured the financial success of Lord Chamberlain's Men during its heyday. Shakespeare's most well-known plays were written and acted during this time, and it is almost certain that the Lord Chamberlain's Men were a powerful, formative influence on the Bard of Avon.

This era in English history was a time of magic and wonder for the art of language, and for English culture as a whole. It has been an exacting work for historians to construct fact out of myth, because records from that time were scarce, or have been lost. The important point to remember, however, is that the most creative writer in the English language was allowed to flourish and prosper for a time, surrounded by those who nourished his creativity. And like many of his great plays, it makes the dramatic ending of such a time even more tragic. From such a rare mix of circumstances, legends are born.

Chapter 1: Playhouses and Playing Companies

To understand Elizabethan theatre, both the terms playhouses and playing companies need some consideration. Spanning the late 16th century through the 17th century in Elizabeth's England, theatres were called playhouses. The group of actors who specifically worked in these buildings were called playing companies. These two terms are often used interchangeably in the historical literature, especially for the most famous examples. A notable playing company was much identified with the physical structure in which it often performed. To speak the name of a playhouse - the Globe for instance - one immediately evoked the name of the players who worked there, the Lord Chamberlain's Men. Often, to reference one was to reference the other. It would seem that the public was very familiar with the names of certain playing companies and, thus, with the playhouses in which that company performed.

There were a handful of specific playhouses and playing companies that dominated the English theatre landscape during this period. The Globe is the most notable playhouse and was the home base of the Lord Chamberlain's Men. Due to the presence of William Shakespeare and the performance of his most famous plays, the Globe has secured a place in history. Pembroke's Men and the Admiral's Men were two other rival playing companies of note. The Admiral's Men were associated with the Rose Theatre, while Pembroke's Men often moved about. Though Pembroke's Men played at the Rose for a time, they eventually secured a contract to work exclusively for the Swan Theatre. Though there was competition between these companies, members of each sometimes moved back and forth between them. This largely had to do with better wages, better opportunities for choice theatre venues, or access to the best playwrights and scripts.

The physical playhouses had a rocky history. At certain points in their timeline, there were several that were highly active and profitable. However, depending on the flow of wealth or the reappearance of the plague, the fortunes of the playhouses plummeted significantly. Difficult and costly to maintain, the playhouses were at the mercy of their wealthy benefactors and the whims of the crowds who paid to see the performances. It was a great risk for any fortune-seeking investor to put his money into a playhouse. During this era in Elizabethan England, actors and playing companies were still primarily owned by the rich. The groups of actors, called players, worked almost exclusively for specific members of the aristocracy. Indeed, this is evidenced by the various names of the playing companies. Each playing company's name always reflected the name or title of the company's wealthy benefactor. This was a common phenomenon and similar situations existed all over Europe during this period. Autonomy for these players and their troupes was a relatively new phenomenon, and had an uncertain future at best. In fact, the players were technically at the beck and call of their benefactors. Their performances for the public were seen as merely rehearsals by officials, and those rehearsals could be shut down at any time.

The profession of acting, and theatre in general, was in the midst of a chaotic sea change in Elizabethan England. Evidenced in various playbills and schedules of the time, players began to peddle their wares outside of the traditional aristocratic audience. Playhouses became more capitalistic and businesslike, and the playing companies began to tour independently across the country. These tours began to leave the country as well, and the playing companies became as famous abroad as they were in England.

While at home in England, however, a troupe of players rarely had carte blanche to perform any play they desired. If the companies were lucky, they had a well-known playwright who worked for them. This sometimes allowed the companies to influence which plays they could perform. Usually, the determination of which performances would see the stage was a mix of the financial needs of the playhouse's benefactor, the desires of the aristocracy, the approval of the Master of Revels, the desires of the Common Council, and popular English opinion. The Master of Revels had final say over all performances in London, and his decisions often involved the Common Council. And the Council itself had an opposing Puritan agenda. It is clear that the playwrights often composed with these various groups in mind. For the playwrights, this became a difficult blend of pleasing multiple groups of people, often whom had differing opinions or agendas. Further intensifying the pressure, the playhouses were forced to contend also with prevailing religious opinions of the time.

Most of the religious traditions of the day treated the actors and their craft as a lewd distraction at best, and as a path to damnation at worst. Although the Anglican Church ruled English spirituality in name, the influence of the Catholic Church was still a powerful factor. It was not an avid supporter of theatre, and its opinions were mirrored by the Puritan factions of the Anglican Church. This posed a grave threat to the playhouses and the players, as the Catholic leadership could be a terrible enemy when it felt thwarted. Both ideologies constantly battled to permanently shut down the playhouses.

The Church of England brought about a great religious and spiritual change for the people and the administrators of Great Britain. Anglicanism was a move away from Catholicism, certainly, but it did not change many core, conservative beliefs. When people began to flock to London to see the great players and their performances, it stoked the fires of conservatism and religious moral outrage. Within the new Anglican movement of the Church of England there lay a powerful faction of Puritanism. This subsection of the Protestants of England regarded excess as a terrible sin, and it was a vice to be avoided at all costs. The bawdy, raucous crowds who attended the plays in the playhouses certainly qualified as excess in their eyes. The churches of the day endlessly preached against this behavior. And these religious institutions had the funds to back their convictions. Beyond the pulpit, they published and circulated pamphlets to proselytize against the theatre. Even though the playhouses were backed by the aristocracy, they could not afford to ignore the voice of the church.

The secular administrators of London also threatened the livelihood of the playing companies. As far as the rulers were concerned, the plays, the players, and those who attended the performances were nothing short of a grave threat to the public interest. The entire atmosphere around each performance was a chaotic carnival. There were crowds of sellers, vendors, rabble rousers, gangs, and thieves. Fights would sporadically break out before and after shows, owing mostly to the consumption of copious amounts of alcohol. Usually such fights pertained to the agendas of rival city gangs. The playhouses always sat next to brothels or taverns and such behavior there was expected. Mostly, it was the large crowds that annoyed the officials of London. Anyone with a nefarious agenda could use the cover of the crowds to perform any illegal deed they could get away with. This included extortion, back alley deals, prostitution, bribery, and even murder. This behavior extended beyond the playhouses as well, as the actors usually relocated to various inns and taverns after the performances. The crowds always followed, and the carnival of civic chaos continued for hours.

Of further concern to the administrators of London was the plague. It could break out without a moment's notice, and often did. A new play performed by such famous actors was certain to draw great crowds. The surging masses of close-knit people were a perfect breeding ground for the sickness. If someone spotted an infected person, it became nearly impossible to disperse the large group of people before the infection spread. Suddenly there would be hundreds of infected, instead of just a few. The fear of infection and the subsequent riots it often caused were no less destructive; this, too, concerned city officials.

Although the cards were certainly stacked against each playing company and the theatres in general, both managed to thrive for several decades. Opinions vary as to how such a fluid group of individuals, within such threatening confines, could survive for so long. But it is certainly due in no small part to the brilliance and unique quality of the playing companies' actors. They were a motley crew of fools, faux princes, writers, charlatans, and lovers who never failed to be intensely entertaining. Such a force was difficult to suppress, even for the religiously dogmatic and authoritarian leaders of the day.

James Burbage and the Origins of The Globe

The life of James Burbage is marked by significant firsts. He was the first private owner of a theatre in Elizabethan England, as well as the first man to build and open such a theatre. Burbage had the privilege, as well, to work under the first tentative laws to protect such interests.

Born around 1535, Burbage spent his early years apprenticed as a carpenter, or joiner, as they were called in his day. He eventually achieved mastery and worked independently in the city of London. These skills would later serve him well, as he became very involved with the building of the playhouse he would come to own. Since funds were limited, it was a boon that he was qualified to build much of the structure himself, and knew who to hire to meet his other construction needs.

In the year 1576, Burbage was the perfect man to fit a perfect need. He was an actor himself, as well as a carpenter, and so knew intimately the problems that actors and playing companies faced. Burbage's playing company, Leicester's Men, began to produce more and more elaborate productions. This situation alone presented many problems with which the shrewd business mind of Burbage wrestled. It took a great deal of labor and time to assemble and disassemble make-shift stages in between productions. Add to this the hassle of moving such equipment from place to place, and Burbage had a problem to solve. It only made sense to him that the solution lay in building a permanent place to stage such productions. Furthermore, he saw the great business opportunity that a permanent venue for his productions could provide. As ever growing crowds appeared to see the plays, many of whom were increasingly wealthy, Burbage knew he sat on a potential gold mine of an idea. His work as a carpenter did not pay as well as he had hoped. He wanted to make more money, and he wanted to do so doing something he loved. Since he already had a career as a traveling actor and, in fact, was the leader of Leicester's Men, it only made sense for him to take the next logical step.

Burbage struggled next with the problem of where to build such a theatre. It was expensive, and nearly impossible to build one in London itself. Although the arts had some umbrella protection from Queen Elizabeth, that protection was far from perfect. Much of the day to day affairs of London were managed by the Common Council, and the Lord Mayor. Neither the Common Council, nor the Mayor, welcomed the art of theatre, let alone a permanent monument to such art. Yet Burbage knew that he must build the structure near enough to London to make the journey there practical for his customers. Two locations presented themselves: Finsbury Field to the north and Bankside to the south. Both were known as locations for recreation.

Bankside had a rather nefarious reputation. It was a place for more base amusements, such as bear-baiting, wrestling, cock fighting and other rough sports. Located near the river's edge, it housed many structures of ill repute, and was known as the locale where the lowest in society gathered. Unfortunately, Bankside already had a reputation as the destination for wandering troupes of actors, and their staged productions. At this time, actors had no place to call a permanent home, even if they entertained the wealthy, so it was only natural that they would gravitate to an inexpensive place to do their work while they waited for their next well-connected patron.

Burbage was very aware of the prevalent opinions held by the officials of London concerning his craft. Bankside had already been targeted by those who felt theatre was wicked and immoral. Many spoke openly about the place, and considered the area little better than a den of iniquity. Building his theatre in Bankside would have been a grave mistake. To do so would only have continued to fuel the notion that his enterprise was sanctioned by a less than divine source. Rather than doom his venture from the start, Burbage instead turned his gaze towards Finsbury Field.

Finsbury was owned by the city of London, and served largely as a public park. Many families used the location as a place to picnic, and the other activities that took place there were considered wholesome in the opinion of city officials. Whether it was the pomp and circumstance of drilling soldiers or the art of the falconer, the Field was a place of respectable leisure activities. And to seal its perfection as the best location for Burbage's theatre, the Field lay within walking distance of the city of London. In 1576, Burbage signed a lease for a portion of property just outside the field, and prepared to secure the funds to build his theatre. He would name it, interestingly enough, the Theatre. He certainly had a right to use this name, as his was the first such building England had ever seen.

James Burbage was not a wealthy man, and the construction of this new theatre cost him a small fortune. He spent every pound he made on it, and placed himself in great debt with money lenders. He even mortgaged the land he leased back to the landowners in order to gather funds for the building of the Theatre. Luck and circumstance favored him, however. Burbage had a wealthy brother-in-law, John Brayne, who secured the bulk of the enormous funds he needed to finish the building.

There are no surviving plans of this original theatre. From the reports of the day, historians know that the building was probably circular, and vast. Several accounts speak of a least a thousand people housed comfortably within. And this fact follows the needs for which Burbage planned. He desired a large space to house the crowds, and he had to design the building to meet the physical and acoustic needs of his playing company. That alone, by necessity, would mean that his Theatre was large. In further evidence, Burbage spent much more on this construction than many others did later on subsequent theatres. It must be assumed that his plans for the building were elaborate.

The building was made of stout wooden timbers. The outside was a mixture of plaster and lime. Historians also report that the building was split into three sections, which surrounded a large common area, called the yard or pit. The three sections, arranged as galleries, would have housed the wealthier patrons. The pit was the catchall. Those unable to pay a larger sum for a gallery seat would be shunted there to mill about, with direct access to the central stage. The pit would always be a crowded place, and subject to chaos. The center stage lay within the pit, and the actors would later discover that they were subject to the whims of the audience if a play went badly. This original Theatre design would inspire many others built after it. The Curtain, for instance, was built only a year later and took its inspiration from Burbage's masterpiece.

James Burbage's original enterprise, the Theatre, operated from 1576 until 1598. It was a huge success, and he made a large sum of money; however, the Theatre had problems, and they mounted up. Burbage's initial land lease locked him at the Theatre's location for 21 years. If the debts to the landlord were not paid before then, the building's title would revert to the landlords. And these same landlords began to demand their share of the daily profits as well, which had been initially promised to them in the lease. Burbage, hounded by debt, knew he would never make any financial headway if he kept the Theatre at its current location. And to make matters worse, Burbage began to quarrel at great length with his brother-in-law over profits as well.

Over the two decades that the Theatre remained in its original location, the fighting between Burbage, the landlords, and his brother-in-law intensified. Others also joined the fray from time to time, demanding their own share of profits based on the most tenuous of claims. James Burbage died in 1597 before he could settle his affairs, and his grand theatre passed to his sons, Cuthbert and Robert. James Burbage's brother-in-law had also died by this time, which left Cuthbert and Robert with only one problem. They had to contend with the landlords' claim on their father's Theatre.

The Lord Chamberlain's Men and Robert Burbage had by this time fled the Theatre's constant financial and ownership issues to perform in another location, a theatre called the Curtain. Not only did Cuthbert face the loss of his father's life's work, the Theatre, but he had lost his father's playing company as well. Cuthbert could stand this state of affairs no longer. He had no choice: he had to save his father's playhouse, and he had to retrieve the playing company his father founded. Time had run out. He had recently received news from a trusted friend that the landlord planned to tear down the Theatre. The landlords planned to use the construction materials for their own projects. Cuthbert wasted no time and contacted his brother, the famous actor Richard Burbage.

Together, Cuthbert and Richard immediately informed the senior members of Lord Chamberlain's Men. The brothers needed help to save their father's theatre, and their family legacy. The company had always been very loyal to their founder, James Burbage, and they agreed to help the Burbage brothers with a bold, and potentially dangerous, plan. They would tear the Theatre down themselves, and remove its parts to a safe location before the landlord could do so. And that is what they did.

On December 28, 1598, the deed was done. Richard and Cuthbert, with 10 others, tore down most of the Theatre and secreted it away to its new home on the Thames River, in Bankside. This region of Bankside, which had been eschewed by James Burbage as initially unfit for his theatre, had become a thriving entertainment center over the years. It already housed several playhouses, namely the Swan, the Bear Garden, and the Rose. And although the original landlords were furious, there was little they could do to stop the Burbage family once they found out what had happened. The standing lease agreement gave the owners of the Theatre, the Burbage brothers, the right to dismantle it.

With advice from members of Lord Chamberlain's Men, including Shakespeare, the architect constructed the new building much differently than the Theatre. The actors had learned design techniques over the years that would enhance the audience's experience of watching a play, and altered the new theatre's design accordingly. By the summer of 1599, the newly designed theatre was finished. It bore a new name as well. The Globe had arrived.

The Globe Theatre

Although James Burbage's vision crafted the modern theatre house as it was known in Elizabethan England, the Globe took that vision even farther. The Globe inspired a whole new business model in the world of acting, and became an astonishing success. Before the Globe, theatres were built by men with financial ambition. James Burbage was such a man. The theatre was conceived as a financial engine, the profits of which benefitted only the owners. When Cuthbert took over his father's business, and rebuilt the theatre, he rebuilt the financial structure as well. No longer did the profits benefit only the owner. Cuthbert and the acting company, Lord Chamberlain's Men, all shared in the theatre's income. This had the dual effect of bringing in some of the most talented actors of the day, as well as ensuring that those actors worked hard to make the theatre a success. The better the theatre's reputation, the more money it made, and the wealthier the actors became.

Initially, the Burbage brothers selected certain individuals to assist them in their vision of a theatre with shared ownership. These individuals would be the first sharers in English theatre history. Not only did they share the profits, but these shareholders were written into the new lease for the building and land as well. The Globe, in its entirety, was now owned by those who worked there. William Shakespeare was one of the first on the list of sharers. His early poetry, play writing, and acting promised to the Globe even greater fame to come. The addition of Richard Burbage and William Kempe secured some of the best acting talent of the day, while Augustine Phillips was a great orator. With the addition of John Heminges, and his financial competence, the deal was set. This line up of the greatest personalities and stars of Elizabethan England ensured that the success of the Globe was a lasting one.

Initially, these individuals held the largest shares of the theatre. But the profits from the Globe trickled down to the entire company in larger amounts than any had ever known. Excellent performances were a given, as everyone who worked there was invested in the success of the theatre. This clever plan also kept the talent together and away from rival playhouses. The dissolution of playing companies, and their constant reorganization, had always made it difficult for any one group of men to make good money for a long period of time.

The Globe is agreed to have been the greatest theatre of its age. Mentioned in numerous historical documents, all comment on its spectacular architectural construction, and the beauty of its form. It was known to be the gold standard by which later theatres were measured. The irony of such reports lay in the fact that there are no surviving plans of the building, or any specific and accurate artistic renderings of it. The few places in which the Globe is depicted in landscape paintings of London from the time, it appears as a vague polygon, or as a semidome. What is certain is that the brilliance of its form, matched to its function, guaranteed the success of its playing company, Lord Chamberlain's Men. Until the Globe closed in 1642, the company never needed to find a new venue for their craft. The company never performed anywhere else except during the coldest winter months, when it moved to the Blackfriars theatre in London. The Globe had large open aired sections, so Lord Chamberlain's Men temporarily relocated their plays until the weather became bearable. The

Blackfriars had been purchased by the Burbage family, as well, so the company simply moved from home to home.

The early years of the Globe are its most noteworthy. It was during this era that the most famous actors of Lord Chamberlain's Men were active, and at the height of their craft. Many of the sharers were legends in their time, and all had amazing gifts that contributed to the Globe's success.

Chapter 2: Notable Performers and Sharers of Lord Chamberlain's Men

The reign of Queen Elizabeth I of England, between the years of 1558 and 1603, is called the Golden Age by historians. This designation is true for this era in acting and theatre, as well. The stages of England were in the midst of significant transition, the likes of which have not been seen again until very modern history. But to understand the prevailing opinions of the time, and the struggles the actors experienced in Elizabeth's England, it is important to briefly discuss the origins of English theatre.

During the centuries before Elizabeth's England, plays and play acting were functions of the Catholic Church. This can be traced back to at least the 12th century. The church often sanctioned what were called Morality Plays or Miracle Plays. A specific story from the Bible, or a moral point, always served as the play's central theme. Acting was a medium solely used to articulate a particular moral or religious point to an audience. Literacy was a rarity among the common people, so it was only natural that acting became a useful medium by which the clergy illustrated their theological points. These plays carried with them great holy significance. Attending them became a sacred duty, much like going to church. The actors in these plays were usually members of the clergy, or their most trusted helpers, and each was educated in the deeper mysteries of religious thought. And while the Morality Plays were rather commonplace, they had become a controversial practice. There were factions in the church who thought such holy stories should only come from the mouths of established clergy, in a pulpit, not a stage.

Gradually, over a century or so, the acting of these plays took on a different form. Despite the gravity of the material, the act of its presentation was a popular form of entertainment, and there were many in need of entertainment. In addition, these plays presented the opportunity to provide paying work, and there were always those in need of jobs. Small groups of actors began to form and travel. They acted out their own versions of morality plays that the people were already familiar with from church. Such productions could spring up anywhere, outside of holy days, and rarely in a church. It was not long before these troupes of players, and their shows, were in high demand.

The church began to censure these productions, and the actors involved, the moment they became aware of them. The clergy handed down new laws. These laws expressly labeled the acting of these plays vulgar, if not heresy itself. The church felt the stories of the holy scripture were its responsibility, and not something that common people should be involved with. Adding fuel to this holy fire, the plays became less and less solemn over the years, as actors improvised and added humor to the stories to make them more entertaining. The church felt this insulted both its sacred mission, and God Himself.

By the time Henry the VIII ascended to the English throne in 1509, this tension between the church and the stage was in full swing. It had been simmering off and on for centuries. The new king's irreverence for the church and church law, however, set precedents that other wealthy elites began to follow. Despite what the church espoused, the king enjoyed a good morality play, with humor, and the king got what he wanted. Others began to follow suit, and wealthy benefactors started to sponsor, and even house, troupes of actors. The religious ban on such entertainment had no choice but to reluctantly loosen its stranglehold. The dark sentiment the church held for such activities remained, however. The church's aversion to theatre would continue to smolder for years, before it flared up again in a new way. For the time being, though, professional actors had some breathing room with which to work.

The field of acting had a new threat to contend with, though, even as the church was forced to ease its restrictions. By the time Elizabeth was crowned in 1559, roving troupes of actors were an established form of entertainment in England. They were still regarded with revulsion by the church, and by many who followed its doctrines, but a man could make a decent living performing his craft on the stage. It was a hard, nomadic life and rarely stable, but it could pay the bills. Troupes moved from town to town, and performed as they could in taverns, inn yards, parks, alleyways, or if they were lucky, in a nobleman's home. The life of an actor was certainly not considered respectable, but it did have its appeal. The prospect of quick money, quick fame, and a quick exit if need be, drew some very interesting people into the acting troupes. But as unstable as an actor's life might have been, even more so was the new reign of an unmarried queen.

Elizabeth was in constant fear of rebellion from multiple factions, and the profession of acting could be used as a medium of attack against her. It was a widespread tactic for political dissidents to use the theatre as a way to drum up support for their goals, especially the goal of unseating a current monarch. Certain plays were used to incite the population against a ruling leader. It had been used to good effect before, and could be used again. For this reason, when Elizabeth took the throne, she instituted new laws that governed the practice of theatre. Acting troupes had to have specific permits to work from local magistrates, and the plays had to be approved ahead of time by those magistrates. Censorship was in full force.

Though the art of theatre experienced new freedoms during Elizabeth's reign, they were far from completely free. Any play that painted the reigning queen or current rulers in an unfavorable light placed the actors and writers in dire jeopardy. There was little a troupe could do to defend themselves in the wake of such suspected actions, and these performers walked a very fine line. The queen's justice was swift, and brutal. It was in this exciting, and dangerous time that the troupe known as Lord Chamberlain's Men worked.

It is very difficult to track various playing companies and their members through history. A lack of historical documentation adds to the mystery of their origins, and that mystery is only deepened by the constant name changing that occurred with these troupes. The members were also known to travel back and forth freely between companies at various times in their careers. Fortunately, the lives of certain core members of Lord Chamberlain's Men can be traced. And it is the inclusion of those specific men that made this playing company famous across Elizabethan England.

William Shakespeare

Shakespeare is the most famous member of Lord Chamberlain's Men, and he was born in Stratford-upon-Avon in 1564. His father was a successful glove maker and his mother came from wealthy landowners, so he did not grow up in a poor home. He seems to have led the typical life of the Elizabethan middle class and was educated in a good school. Later, he was married at the age of 18 in what was probably an arranged marriage. He left his wife and children alone for long intervals of time, so it can be assumed that married life did not agree with him. It is difficult to say for certain what drove him away, but after his marriage and the birth of his children, he disappeared from history until 1592. When he surfaced, his plays had begun to show up in the playbills of London. His theatrical creations were produced for the stage and history shows that Shakespeare quickly began making a name for himself as a playwright, and as an actor.

It is assumed that Shakespeare's career in theatre began in the 1580s. This is a safe assumption, and seems to fit the timeline. There are surviving articles in London publications that mention him and his works during these years. By 1592, he was a controversial figure in the publications of London, and his name is often mentioned. He was accused of being a hack, and not fit literary company for his more educated contemporaries. Christopher Marlowe was a very famous playwright in London at this time, and there were many critics who felt that Shakespeare's own writing could not hope to compare with Marlowe's work. When Marlowe was murdered in a tavern in 1593, the comparisons between the two playwrights ended, and Shakespeare wrote freely without the burden of further comparisons.

Shakespeare was an established and ranked member of Lord Chamberlain's Men by 1594. Because Shakespeare had been given a large share of the playing company years before, they always considered his advice regarding future decisions for the troupe. Richard Burbage had made a brilliantly successful decision in including Shakespeare as one of the sharers, and the Bard's genius paid off. Shakespeare's plays alone made the troupe very famous.

The Bard of Avon worked as both a writer and an actor. He was paid for his performances on stage, and received incremental income during his playwriting process. Playwrights at that time were often paid small sums for each act of a play they finished, rather than a larger sum for the play as a whole. As a sharer in Lord Chamberlain's Men, Shakespeare also received a portion of the profits gained from those who attended the performances at the Globe. It was a lucrative bargain for all involved. The company founded by Burbage's father had the exclusive right to perform Shakespeare's plays from 1594 until 1642. These plays saw most of their production in the Globe Theatre. But Lord Chamberlain's Men also performed for Queen Elizabeth on many occasions. Her patronage alone secured the company a great deal of fame and fortune. Even after the death of Queen Elizabeth in 1603, the troupe's notoriety remained undiminished. King James I, the successor to Elizabeth, renewed the troupe's playing license and took them as his personal entertainers. The company's name changed to the King's Men that same year to reflect this new royal patronage, and Shakespeare remained a valued member.

History shows that Shakespeare was an actor as well as a writer. It is certain that he performed in the productions he wrote, but exactly whom he played, or when, is less certain. He is rumored to have played Hamlet's ghost at one point, although this is unproven. It does seem to be a minor, but important, role that would have suited Shakespeare. With great actors at his disposal, like William Kempe or Richard Burbage, it is unlikely that Shakespeare would have ever starred in one of his own plays. As the writer, though, it follows that Shakespeare would have filled in for the smaller roles as needed.

Shakespeare had access to others in the troupe more specifically suited to the parts he wrote. Richard Burbage, for example, was very famous for his nuanced portrayal of complicated characters. He was often cast to play the leading characters in *Othello*, *Hamlet* or *King Lear*. Similarly, William Kempe was known as one of England's best comedians. It would not have been out of place to see him on stage playing the funny role of Falstaff from Shakespeare's history play, *Henry IV*. The collaboration between the writer of a play and specific actors does not stretch the imagination. It was an asset for a playwright to consider his primary actors whenever he wrote a piece, and he wrote with the casting of those actors in mind. Collaboration between stage writers was normal behavior in Elizabethan England. It is commonly assumed by historians and biographers that Shakespeare co-wrote his last few plays with John Fletcher. Fletcher succeeded Shakespeare as the lead writer for Lord Chamberlain's Men after Shakespeare's death. Fletcher had collaborated with others himself when his wrote his first plays.

Shakespeare's plays were published one at a time, in small pamphlet form, and they were circulated in London during his career. Publication was rare and costly, so usually only the most famous or wealthy playwrights could afford to publish their work. Although expensive, publication guaranteed a playwright's visibility and fame. Shakespeare had become wealthy as an actor, and he used part of his wealth to ensure that his current plays were accessible. The first 14 or so were published anonymously, and did not bear Shakespeare's name as the author. The rest of these published pamphlets, called quartos, did bear his name in print. Shakespeare's name was published in various forms, spellings, and hyphenations over the years of his life. This spurred a later controversy in the 19th century as to whether Shakespeare was indeed the real author of the plays which bear his name. It is a controversy which persists to this day, despite the fact that no one questioned Shakespeare's authorship during his life, or for hundreds of years after. By the time of his retirement in 1611, and his death in 1616, Shakespeare had secured his reputation.

England's great Bard is recognized throughout the world as the father of the modern play. His words changed the flavor of English discourse and his phrases still salt and pepper modern conversations today. Shakespeare's plays continue to grace the stages of the world and his stories have evolved into a thousand different varieties. Whether stage, film, television, or books, Shakespeare's original themes crop up time and again. It is certain that he will continue to influence drama and comedy, in all their forms, for a long time to come.

Richard Burbage

Richard Burbage was born in 1567, in Stratford-upon-Avon. He and Cuthbert were the sons of the founder of Lord Chamberlain's Men, James Burbage. Richard grew up with the actor father who owned England's first theatre. It then comes as no surprise that Richard and his brother, Cuthbert, both became actors. Although his early years of acting are not well documented, historians know that Richard was well established in the theatre scene by the time he reached his early 20s. His early career is a fine example of the jostling that often went on between acting companies. Richard worked with the Admiral's Men, Lord Strange's Men, and the Earl of Pembroke's Men. He moved back and forth between these companies within a few years of each other.

Richard had an uncanny knack for playing leading roles, and he played them often. The leading roles that Shakespeare wrote were difficult and long, with a great deal of emotional depth. Richard acted those roles with a fluid ease and his skill was in great demand. Edward Alleyn was the only other actor of the time who was able to accomplish such a feat. Consequently, Richard became the perfect addition to a company that routinely produced the plays of William Shakespeare, and Burbage joined Lord Chamberlain's Men not long after his father's death.

Richard Burbage became one of the most important sharers of Lord Chamberlain's Men. He and his brother were tangled for years in petty legal problems after they dismantled the Theatre. His family also owned the Blackfriars Theatre. It was this smaller theatre, purchased by his father, which housed Lord Chamberlain's Men in the winter months. Both buildings were inherited by the brothers, and each presented its share of trials. It is a testament to Richard's acting skill that he was able to juggle the complex management of two theatres, while his acting elevated Lord Chamberlain's Men to the status of legend. Fortunately, Richard's brother, Cuthbert, was himself a good actor, and had business savvy as well. Between them both, they were able to settle the largest of the legal disputes, and their business continued uninterrupted. Without the skill of these two brothers, the history of Lord Chamberlain's Men and the Globe would have been a far different story.

As an actor, Richard was in high demand for most of his life. Although his ultimate allegiance lay with the Globe and his own acting company, Richard acted in other theatres. Motivated by extra money, or propelled by professional pride, Burbage starred in several productions away from his home theatre. He graced various stages, and acted from the great works of Shakespeare's contemporary playwrights, Ben Jonson and John Marston. These writers considered Burbage's skill as an actor of tragedies to be superb. His exceptional performances elevated their own work in a mutually beneficial partnership. They owed no small part of their own good fortune to him.

Of the three genres of Shakespeare's plays, tragedy was considered the hardest for an actor to pull off effectively. If the actor performed without depth, the tragedy had no emotional punch and failed to move an audience to feel the grief of the characters. If the same role were overacted, then the play became melodramatic and unrealistic. Burbage's portrayal of King Lear, for example, was perfect. Lear's character was a difficult role to play, and the story ends in a catastrophe. King Lear goes insane, and ultimately dies. It took an actor of exceeding skill to pull off this performance in such a way that the audience became both sympathetic for the tragic character, but repulsed by his actions. Richard Burbage was a natural method actor. He could assume the mannerisms and personality of each role he played. His ability to shape shift into his characters never failed to impress, and his performances were often a topic of conversation for weeks in London.

Due to his popularity at the time, there are a few amusing stories that have survived the years regarding Richard's personal exploits. One of the more colorful of these tales spoke of a female admirer who fell in love with Burbage after she witnessed his portrayal of King Richard III on stage. She asked him to meet her later in her private rooms, after the play. She also requested that he dress as the famous king. It is said that Shakespeare overheard the conversation between Burbage and the unknown lady, and left the performance early in order to reach her first. The two actor friends often enjoyed such competition for the affections of their female fans. Burbage, dressed as requested, later went to see his lady friend. When he reached her door, he announced dramatically that Richard III had appeared as requested. He was too late. Shakespeare, who answered from inside the room, called out that William the Conqueror had already arrived.

For actors like Richard Burbage, performing for royalty was the greatest privilege. These performances secured both wealth and prestige for the acting company, and such jobs were only given to the most talented actors in a troupe. Burbage was listed among the actors in Lord Chamberlain's Men who performed for both Queen Elizabeth I, and her successor, James I. One of the performances for Queen Elizabeth took place in Greenwich, in 1594. Both are also listed in 1604 as having performed for the royal procession of James I and his family. The records noted that the actors received yards of costly red cloth as payment for their services.

Most actors of Burbage's notoriety eventually retired and enjoyed their wealth during their old age. Richard Burbage did not. He continued with Lord Chamberlain's Men until his death in 1619. He had achieved great fame and fortune in his day, but had little of that fortune left when he died. He was never particularly good with money, and had only managed to purchase and retain a small estate. He left the house, and what remained of his funds, to his family.

William Kempe

William Kempe appeared in the London theatre community around 1585. Little is known of his early life, but by the 1580s he was an actor in the company known as Leicester's Men. He worked with James Burbage and later joined Lord Chamberlain's Men in 1594, after the Leicester's Men were dissolved as a troupe. He did not stay with Lord Chamberlain's Men for very long, just a few years, but the addition of his skill helped make the new company famous. Kempe had already made a reputation for himself as a legendary clown and comedian, and his inclusion in any production drew great crowds. He became an icon for many who followed after him. Most of the comedic characters created during this time were written specifically for Kempe.

One of Kempe's greatest performances was the character, Falstaff, who was written into three of Shakespeare's plays. Falstaff is a fat, cowardly knight who is vain and boastful. The Elizabethan people found large, stupid characters to be very funny, and Kempe excelled at playing this buffoon on stage. The role sealed his reputation as a master comedian, and insured that the theatre was full of paying customers each time he performed it. He also played Dogberry, from *Much Ado About Nothing*, a role which pokes fun at imbecilic police officers, and Peter from *Romeo and Juliet*.

Kempe was an excellent dancer as well. He incorporated dance and physical comedy into his roles. He often contorted his face in strange ways, or stumbled around on the stage in a drunken parody. These physical antics delighted Elizabethan crowds, especially if they ranged from oafish to graceful. His stumbles always ended with a flourish, and moved from clumsy to graceful in a fluid dance routine that brought roars from the crowd every time. He also excelled at the Elizabethan stage jig.

Elizabethan crowds loved a jig, and it was performed at the end of each play. The crowd awaited the improvised dance with tense anticipation. Each jig had a loose plot line, usually announced in a dramatic way by a fellow actor just before the dancer appeared. The plot could be political or serious in tone, but it always contained some form of satire. The dance itself was at times slow, then fast, and included bouts of singing. The dancer could be very bawdy, and was encouraged to make lewd jokes while he twirled about. Other actors would join the dance, and it often ended with the entire cast of the play on stage. The act of the jig performed a cathartic role for the audience, and allowed the crowd to blow off some steam. This was especially effective if the play they had just witnessed was a tense drama. The jig often whipped the audience into a rowdy frenzy, so it was frowned upon by the moral and religious authorities of the time. In 1612, there was formal attempt to suppress such jigs, but due to the dance's popularity, the measure failed. Kempe was a master of such improvised comedic dances.

Kempe left Lord Chamberlain's Men suddenly in 1599. The exact reason is unknown, but historians speculate that he and Shakespeare fought over Kempe's inability to follow a script. Much of Kempe's comedy was spontaneous and disruptive, and he enjoyed improvisation. This continued behavior annoyed the company itself, and Shakespeare in particular. Shakespeare seemed to later reference his fallout with Kempe in certain lines from *Hamlet*, which discussed clowns who are too fond of improvisation.

In 1600, Kempe performed his opus for the people of London. In his memoirs, he called the performance his Nine Days of Wonder. He danced all the way from London to Norwich, nearly a hundred miles away. The event was a media spectacle and was as dramatic a performance as any actor could have wanted. He briefly returned to stage in 1601, but disappeared two years later from the records. He is thought to have died in 1603, the same year one of the worst outbreaks of the plague hit London.

Augustine Phillips

The early life of Augustine Phillips is another historical mystery. The lack of records makes it difficult for biographers to track his early years. He first appears in documents dating close to 1590. By that time he was an established member of the Lord Strange's Men, although he acted with several companies. He is mentioned in several documents that issued permission for the troupes to tour. He probably joined Lord Chamberlain's Men after 1592. The patron of Lord Strange's Men had died, and it left the company without a royal protector. The troupe was forced to disband and Phillips joined Richard Burbage's company.

The circumstances around Phillips' origins are mysterious, but his position with Lord Chamberlain's Men is not. He was one of the core sharers. He was present in 1598 when the Globe was built, and had established himself as a solid actor. Because he was a sharer in the Globe, it is reasonable to assume that Burbage and the others counted him as an asset. His share in the Globe made him a very wealthy man, and he was one of the first examples of how lucrative a career the theatre had become in Elizabethan England. History also recorded him as a great orator. In 1601, Phillips' skill played a key role in one of the very few scandals to hit Lord Chamberlain's Men.

Queen Elizabeth I had many enemies. Her reign, though called the Golden Age of England, was one rife with plots to dethrone her. The acting companies of the time were often embroiled in these plots, though unwittingly. In 1601, the Earl of Essex schemed to overthrow his queen. The circumstances around the plot shocked the people at the time, as the Earl was counted as one of the queen's favorite courtiers. He had fought with her, though, presumably as a lover, and the quarrel had gone very sour. Elizabeth stripped him of his monopoly in wine production, and had nearly made him a pauper. In a rage, he fortified his estates and prepared to march through London in order to force an audience with Elizabeth. To bolster public opinion of this bold move, he hired Lord Chamberlain's Men to perform the play, *Richard II*, the night before his march. The play spoke of the need for old monarchy to be replaced by newer blood. The coup failed, and the Earl was later executed. An official inquiry was launched immediately. The actors of Lord Chamberlain's Men were called before the officials of London to answer for their part in Essex's rebellion. If they were found guilty, they faced execution as well.

Phillips was sent to speak before the Council as the troupe's representative. He argued passionately that the company had no idea of the Earl's plot, and had only taken the job because they had been paid a large sum of money. He also explained that the company thought the play was old and out of date, and not worthy of further productions. Phillips' oratory must have swayed the court, as the company received absolutely no punishment for their role in the Essex rebellion. In fact, they were invited to perform for the queen herself the day before Lord Essex was executed.

One of the longest standing members, Augustine Phillips remained with the company for many years. He died in 1605, and his will revealed a great deal about him. He left large sums of money to his family, of course, but also to his fellow actors. He held them in high regard. His will also held a surprise for a little regarded group in the Globe: the common laborers. He left them a significant sum and asked that they split it equally.

John Heminges

Born in 1556, John Heminges became the primary money manager for Lord Chamberlain's Men. Every successful acting company in Elizabethan England handled a great deal of money. Without a successful manager for that wealth, it is unlikely that any troupe would have lasted very long. John Heminges served that role in Shakespeare's company, and he was very qualified to do so.

When he was 12 years old, Heminges traveled to London to apprentice with the Grocers. In the 16th century, Grocers were a powerful guild in England. Called a Livery Company, the grocers' full title was Worshipful Company of Grocers. In charge of spice quality, and the standardization of weights and measures, they were one of the most influential trade associations of the time. Heminges apprenticed with them for nine years, and became a full member by the time he reached the age of 21. This apprenticeship assured that his knowledge of management and finances was sound.

He married the daughter of an actor when he was 32, and began to make his mark in the world of theatre. He worked with Augustine Phillips in Lord Strange's Men in 1593, and joined Lord Chamberlain's Men in 1594. Most of his trail is recorded through financial records, as he received funds from benefactors during the troupe's tours. He also became the middle man between the company and the Master of Revels of London. This official oversaw the plays and the playing companies of the time. Each performance had to be approved by the Revel Master's office, and Heminges's signature on the documents testified to his role as the company's manager in London.

Heminges had many financial irons in the fire during his career. He owned the alehouse next to the Globe, which was a lucrative venture, and he later served as a trustee for the purchase of Shakespeare's home. John Heminges juggled two careers at once, and did so to great effect. He remained a grocer in high standing during his lifetime, and took on many young apprentices in this field. These same young men were also in high demand in theatre at the time, employed to play the roles of women on stage. Since females were not allowed to be a part of the profession of acting, troupes would employ prepubescent boys to take their place in the theatres' productions. The names of Heminges' apprentices appeared in later playbills for Lord Chamberlain's Men. These apprentices learned the art of acting, while they also learned the duties of a Grocer. Heminges taught them the skills needed for the dual career that he himself enjoyed.

Although he was more intimately involved with the playing company's finances, Heminges did perform on the stage. Most notably, he played in several productions written by Ben Jonson. He was often cast alongside Shakespeare for Jonson's work, and may have played in Jonson's *Volpone* at the Globe in 1606. Heminges died in 1630, and passed his shares in the Globe to his son. Although Heminges was not a famous actor, his love for the craft and his friendship for his fellow actors became immortalized in his effort to publish Shakespeare's plays after the death of the Bard. Without the publication of those famous Folios, funded by Heminges and fellow actor Henry Condell, it is impossible to say how well Shakespeare's greatest works would have weathered the long years of history.

Henry Condell

The lives of most of the Elizabethan actors are obscured. Historians have worked tirelessly to piece together cohesive biographies out of mere scraps of written information. Henry Condell's life is no different. At best guess, with available birth records, he was born in 1576 to a fisherman and his wife. There is little concrete information about his early years, although much can be speculated. Nearly all of the early years of actors in Elizabethan England were spent apprenticed to some craft, while at the same time they learned the actor's art. Whether they were the children of actors, or felt their own calling to the stage in later life, they always appeared in theatre records as already established. In 1596, when Condell is first mentioned in the official records due to his marriage, he had already become a presence in the London theatre world. At the age of 20, he was an actor.

It is possible that his career began as one of the young male child actors so eagerly sought at this time. His parents were poor, so an early recruitment into the theatre for extra money made sense. It is thought that one of his first roles was in Richard Tarlton's *The Seven Deadly Sins*. Condell's first name, Henry, appears on the cast list. If this is true, then he was an actor in 1590, at the age of 14. He would have worked for the Lord Strange's Men, and thus would have known John Heminges and Augustine Phillips. History records that Heminges and Condell were great friends, so this historical speculation is sound. Regardless of how he first got to the stage, he moved through the ranks of actors quickly.

Henry Condell was recorded on the cast list for a performance of a Ben Jonson play in 1598. The Lord Chamberlain's Men performed *Every Man in His Humour* at the Curtain Theatre. Condell was definitely a member of the company at this time. This performance was one of the last the company staged before the Globe opened in 1599. At this time, Richard and Cuthbert Burbage were deep in consideration over who to bring in as Globe sharers. Condell was one of the first they picked. He is again recorded on the cast list for Ben Jonson's sequel, *Every Man Out of His Humour*, which was performed at the Globe in 1599. He also appeared in cast lists in 1603 and 1610.

Condell's career with Lord Chamberlain's Men was long and profitable. When he died in 1627, his will disbursed a rather large estate. Condell is best known, however, for the collection and publication of the plays of William Shakespeare into a large folio after Shakespeare's death. He helped arrange them into a single volume, which was later called the First Folio. He and his friend, John Heminges, split the cost of the First Folio's publication in 1623. Both wanted to ensure that the writing of their friend remained in circulation. It is from this publication, and the subsequent reprint in the Second Folio of 1632, that most of Shakespeare's work has survived.

Thomas Pope

Thomas Pope was one of the original eight sharers for Lord Chamberlain's Men. He is another Elizabethan actor about whose early life almost nothing is known for certain. His role as a sharer was shorter lived than the rest of the members, so it is assumed that he started as one of the older actors of Lord Chamberlain's Men. He appeared in the same production of *The Seven Deadly Sins* in 1591 that featured Richard Burbage, Augustine Phillips, and Edward Alleyn. By then, he was part of an existing acting company. Alleyn and Burbage both starred in this production, so it is clear that Pope worked with the greatest actors of the age. His skill must have been considerable.

A great outbreak of the plague in London in 1593 forced the theatres to shut down for a time. Edward Alleyn organized a touring troupe, made of actors from Lord Strange's Men and his own company, the Admiral's Men. Pope traveled and acted with them until the theatres reopened in June of 1594. Fortune then smiled upon Pope. That same year Lord Chamberlain's Men reassembled. He was asked to join them then and, four years later, he shared in the new theatre venture called the Globe. His role in Lord Chamberlain's Men involved governing the troupe's finances. His name is well documented as having received funds for performing for the royal court. Only a trusted member of the acting troupe would have been given such a responsibility. Pope probably worked alongside John Heminges, the troupe's most important financial manager, in this capacity.

When Lord Chamberlain's Men changed their name to the King's Men in 1603, Pope was no longer a member. Biographers assume that he was retired by then. He died later that year and left his theatre shares, which were considerable, to a lady named Mary Clark. Little is known of her. Pope had shares in both theatres, the Curtain and the Globe, and his gift of them to Mary Clark must have made her wealthy.

William Sly

The exact date and place of William Sly's birth is unknown. Like so many from this period, his origins are a mystery. Biographers surmise that Sly joined Lord Chamberlain's Men first as a hired hand. He later transitioned into acting. This was not unusual for the time, as many members of a troupe often wore numerous hats, whether it was laborer, actor, or manager. His first recorded appearance as an actor occurred as another cast member from the 1591 play, *The Seven Deadly Sins*. This particular play served biographers as a touchstone to find several of Lord Chamberlain's Men a place in history.

Sly appeared again in the records in 1594, when Lord Chamberlain's Men reassembled. He became a core sharer of the company by the time the Globe was finished in 1599, so he had proven his worth as an actor. It was not until 1605 that he actually became a sharer of the theatre itself. He appeared in a production of *Hamlet* in 1602, and in several performances of plays by Ben Jonson. His exact role in Lord Chamberlain's Men is uncertain, but he had the confidence of the inner circle.

In 1605, when Augustine Phillips died, William Sly was one of the executors of his will. Sly also had shares in the Blackfriars Theatre, and was with the company when it became the King's Men in 1603. William Sly died in 1608, shortly after his investiture in the Blackfriars. His will left large sums of money to fellow actors. He had no direct heirs that were named, and his shares of the theatres were split among the remaining shareholders.

Robert Armin

Robert Armin was born in 1563. His father was a successful tailor, so Armin grew up with wealth and influence, and was well educated. He did not follow his father's career path, however, and instead was apprenticed to a family friend. After 1581, Armin worked as a goldsmith within their guild. The position would have lead him to a far different future had fate not intervened. Rather than become a goldsmith, Armin became a comedian.

Armin began to write small comedies. But the end of his goldsmith apprenticeship in 1592, he was already well known for those comedies. One day he was sent on an errand to collect a debt owed to his master. He traveled to an inn owned by the Queen's jester and personal comedian, Richard Tarlton. Armin had trouble getting the gentleman housed at the inn to pay his debt, and in his frustration, he wrote witty comments about the man in chalk on the walls of the inn. The queen's comedian, Tarlton, noticed the written jests and was impressed. He asked Armin to apprentice with him, and provided an outlet for Armin's comedy.

By the late 1590s, Armin was an established stage actor. He performed for the troupe, the Chandos Company, and made a name for himself as a great comedian. His skill rivaled that of William Kempe, and he specialized in acting the role of clowns. Armin's superb education, however, gave his roles a depth that few could match. His on-stage clowning moved in range from witless fool to philosophical madman.

Armin is thought to have joined Lord Chamberlain's Men in 1600, after the removal of William Kempe from the troupe. Armin published two of his many works on comedy, *Fool Upon Fool* and *Quips upon Questions*, that same year and was considered the authority in London on the craft. He elevated the position of "the fool" on stage. No longer was the role merely a silly distraction for audiences. The fool became a celebrated character. Many of the roles for the fool that Shakespeare later wrote were almost certainly written specifically for Robert Armin. He played the role of Feste in *Twelfth Night*, and the Fool in *King Lear*. By the time he died in 1615, the role of the clown had secured its place in theatre history. The clown became a serious staple of the stage.

Chapter 3: Rival Playing Companies

When they first formed, the Lord Chamberlain's Men worked in a ruthless atmosphere in London. They were in constant fear of losing their fame and status. Although they were the best acting company in England, they had to be wary of rivals. During the Renaissance in Elizabeth's England, many playing companies existed. All of them traveled around the countryside, looking for a paying audience. As actors came together to seek their fortunes, these companies formed quickly. They often dissolved just as rapidly. During this time, the acting profession transitioned from a field of unsteady jobs into a lucrative career that could bring great fortune. No longer were actors just a group of poor individuals, with little talent, who earned a few pennies. The actors were educated, well trained, seasoned and ambitious. Consequently, it was a very competitive field. Actors competed for the best playhouses, the most lavish costumes, the largest audiences, the most talented playwrights, and the wealthiest benefactors. There was virtually no aspect of an actor's life that was not a race to be the best.

This career came with hazards as well. One bad play or one bad performance could doom a company, especially if that company's benefactor became displeased. And all actors worked within the tense atmosphere generated by the puritan beliefs of the officials of London, and the Lord Mayor. Companies could not avoid his influence since London was the major center for an actor's trade, and he controlled London. His beliefs were not unique to him and the city he controlled. Puritanism had spread throughout England like a brushfire, inflaming many of the wealthy with a righteous anger against any sort of excess. Despite this brewing storm of difficult times, a rival for Lord Chamberlain's Men emerged.

The Admiral's Men formed around 1576, the same year that James Burbage opened his playhouse, The Theatre. The Admiral's Men had first gained the financial backing of Earl Charles Howard, and they were originally known as Lord Howard's Men. When Howard secured the title of Lord High Admiral, the company changed its name to reflect his new status. The Admiral was a champion for theatre, and in him the company had found a powerful ally. In 1584, the puritanical Lord Mayor of London fought to close the play houses and end the profession of theatre for good. Using the threat of a plague outbreak, he and his supporters had tried this tactic before with some success. His movement to brand the profession of acting as unfit for the puritans of English society grew stronger by the year. Admiral Howard was one of the few influential voices who helped persuade Queen Elizabeth to stop the Mayor. She intervened, and the theatres remained open. This would not be the last time that the Admiral's Men were threatened by the Lord Mayor, however. In 1589 he used his power and influence to halt the performances of both the Admiral's Men and another company, Lord Strange's Men. The Master of the Revels did not appreciate their choice of plays, and the Lord Mayor pounced on any excuse to hamper the profession of theatre in London. Both companies were forced to move to the Theatre, James Burbage's first enterprise, and remained there for a time. James Burbage's son, Richard, had just begun his career in acting. This was the only time he acted alongside Edward Alleyn, who would later become his greatest rival on the stage.

The Admiral's Men had several important members who contributed to its fame and success. The acting company's crown jewel was Edward Alleyn. He was generally regarded as the greatest actor in England. His career was established by 1583, and he was listed as one of the actors for the Earl of Worcester. He worked for many companies over the years, but when he married the daughter of Phillip Henslowe in 1592, his relationship with the Admiral's Men was cemented. Henslowe was the wealthy theatre owner of the Rose, which became the center of Alleyn's work for many years. Henslowe supported the Admiral's Men in many ways. He first gave them a home in the Rose, until the Fortune theatre was built in 1600. Henslowe kept a very detailed journal of his financial exploits from this era, and it is regarded as an invaluable source of theatrical historical knowledge.

Alleyn's marriage to Henslowe's daughter opened many financial doors for him. He became Henslowe's partner in the Rose, and in nearly all of Henslowe's later theatrical ventures. The two owned several theatres in London, including the Paris Garden and the Fortune. The Admiral's Men had numerous venues in which to work, and they took advantage of all of them. Alleyn and Henslowe were master entrepreneurs, and had investments in other entertainments as well. They owned taverns, bear baiting pits and several London brothels. Alleyn quickly became very wealthy, and even became a favorite actor of the Queen. She personally requested him on numerous occasions, and asked for him to return to the stage after he retired. He declined, and only returned briefly in 1604, after her death. Alleyn later used much of his wealth to buy a great estate that secured his place in English history. He founded Dulwich College, a private school for boys, which is still in operation. Throughout his career, Alleyn vied with Richard Burbage for the position of England's favorite actor. But, before his death, it was Christopher Marlowe who vied with Shakespeare to be England's greatest playwright.

Marlowe wrote with exceptional skill. He purposefully wrote his lead roles with Alleyn in mind. The combination of such a talented writer working with a legendary method actor took London by storm. Marlowe and Alleyn dazzled audiences at the Rose, just as Richard Burbage's performances of Shakespeare's characters drew great crowds at the Globe. Alleyn was such a marvelous actor that it is often speculated that Marlowe's greatest plays, *Doctor Faustus* and *Tamburlaine*, may not have been so legendary without Alleyn to play the lead role.

After the Fortune Theatre was built in 1600, the Admiral's Men took it as their new home. In 1603, the company changed its name to Prince Henry's Men, to reflect their new patronage from the royal line of King James I. The new prince died early, however, and it was a tragedy that seemed to presage the end of the acting company that bore his name. In 1621 the Fortune Theatre burned to the ground. It was a total loss, and many of the company's stock plays and costumes were also consumed by the fire. Edward Alleyn funded the rebuilding of the theatre in 1623, but he never recaptured its early success. The company continued to perform until 1631 when it finally collapsed. The members left, joined new troupes, and the Fortune became a shadow of its former self. New companies entered the Fortune, but none could ever achieve the prestige of the disbanded Admiral's Men.

Chapter 4: Performances

Setting the Stage

An understanding of the performances of Shakespeare's company, Lord Chamberlain's Men, requires an examination of the Elizabethan audience. It is also important to review the atmosphere around a typical performance. As much as ten percent of London's population attended plays in the late 1500s. Whether the plays were performed in playhouses or staged in the common rooms of taverns, Londoners considered drama to be a favored leisure activity. These audiences consisted not just of the middle class and wealthy, but of the poor as well. Any given audience of this time was a representative mix of all of London's population. A writer and his actors had many variables to consider whenever they crafted a performance. Some of the most basic factors included those who attended the plays, the places where the plays were performed, the timing of performances, and the sociopolitical views of the time. Each performance was a clever orchestration by the actors and the writers, planned with complexity. The plays were not just random stories, acted to amuse a population in order to make money. The stories often acted as social commentary, which contained religious and political positions. Each performance, which sometimes contained elements from ancient history, expected to teach its audience a lesson through reflection. The plays that Shakespeare wrote, and the performances of any good playing company, held a mirror up to their audience. It forced the thinking observer to regard himself, and to consider his place in the world.

There was inherent danger in this activity. Though the plays were expected to be witty and engaging, great caution became necessary whenever they were written. The playwright first had to be very careful about the subject matter, or about whom, he wrote. Bruising the honor or ego of someone important could lead to trouble. Further complicating the process, the writer and the players had to consider not just what was written, but what an audience member could infer from what was written. Playwrights engaged in a dangerous game of guessing how a play would be received. Mobs could break out among the general audience if they were angered, and an actor could be pulled down from the stage and hurt. But the actors and writers also feared a far more an insidious threat. They had to be certain that their shows did not offend the powerful. Freedom of speech did not exist during this time. At any moment, a city official who became offended could censor a play, end a performance, or even permanently close a playhouse. This was serious enough, but the consequences became dire for a writer or actor who dared to offend the ruling aristocracy. The offender could find himself immediately imprisoned, or even executed. Every performance became a precarious dance between being clever and entertaining, without offending those who were in power. A firm hierarchy ruled the stages of London in Elizabethan England. This hierarchy was echoed in the construction of the theatres themselves.

The Globe was an open-air building, used primarily for summer and mild weather performances. Two large staircases on either side of the building led to the upper three galleries. As a whole, the galleries were reserved for the wealthy and the elite. For the most powerful lords and ladies, there existed an enclosed space called the Lords' Room. The rest sat, arranged according to their influence and place in society, in the surrounding tiers. Their admission to the show paid not only for cushioned seats, but to have the best vantage point, and to be above the poorer crowds that milled below. Within the galleries lords, ladies, merchants, and officials all mingled together. The scene was similar to one that could be witnessed in the courts of the royal leaders of England. The elite would mingle, visit friends and relatives, make alliances, broker deals, or amuse themselves with witty banter. Many would place wagers on the performances of certain actors, or on whether a play would please or anger certain officials. The whispered sounds of velvet and lace could be heard amongst the laughter, and the wealthy donned their most spectacular clothing. Jewels twinkled amidst curled wigs of perfumed hair as unmarried women sought to catch the eye of an unmarried lord. It was all a polite sort of chaos, which reflected in tone the physical spectacle below them.

The area below the galleries was called the yard, or more commonly, the pit. It was a large open field that surrounded the main stage. For the price of one penny, hundreds of people who could not afford the better seats above wandered about. They were tightly packed into the space, and there were no seats. The gyrating crowds here were a spectacle for those who occupied the upper gallery. The gentry called them the groundlings. A groundling was a term used to mean a small, open mouthed fish. This term was first openly used to reference the audience in the pit during a performance of *Hamlet* in 1600. The actor who played Hamlet called the people before him groundlings, and it certainly made sense to those who heard it. The mass of open-mouthed faces before him resembled a sea of gaping fish. It was a sight to behold, as bizarre as it was dangerous.

The pit was a chaotic mix of human behavior. Drinking, loud laughter, verbal and physical arguments, and lewd acts were just a few of the sights a lord could witness from above. Food sellers plied their trade, while unmarried men shoved and jockeyed for position next to a desired woman. Children and dogs pushed their ways through the legs of adults, as thieves lurked about, ready to cut away a man's money pouch and flee. It would not have been a surprise to see an intimate couple engaged not far from a crowd of men who caroused and cheered on a vicious fight. The crowds were fickle, and no behavior was taboo. It was not unknown for the groundlings to boo and hiss, if they disliked a particular actor or his role, or to throw nuts and fruit on stage. Fortunately, however, this was not a common occurrence. Reports of this activity, within official records of the time, were probably inflated to support the closure of London's theatres. The antics of the groundlings were certainly used to fuel the anti-theatre rhetoric of conservatives and Puritans alike.

The pre-performance stage flurried with activity. Hired hands brought out props, arranged furniture and cloth drapes, and prepared the elevated platform where the actors would perform. At the same time, wealthier guests often paid a fee to visit the actors on the stage itself. For a good sum of money, audience members could rent a stool and sit and chat with the actors before the show began. They would admire the actors' costumes or skill, or the actor himself. Sometimes a well-known troupe player would begin to recite lines from his more famous plays. These visits were used by actors to secure the favors of a wealthy patron, or to book later private performances at a large estate.

The price of a theatre ticket in Elizabethan England paid for many delights and experiences for the senses. The theatre goers of London gravitated to the stages for more than just the performances themselves. The theatres had a carnival atmosphere, as distracting and exciting as anyone could wish for. The unrestrained energy released before, during and after each show functioned as a cathartic experience for everyone present.

Specific Performances

When Shakespeare first joined Lord Chamberlain's Men, he brought with him the talents of a master playwright. No longer did the company have to beg for the opportunity to perform the plays of others, or pay the fees required to act from the scripts written by Marlowe and Jonson. They had a house playwright, and evidenced from the bulk of Shakespeare's output at this time, they certainly took advantage of it. An examination of which plays were performed during this time is a direct view into Elizabethan culture. They were written to address current political, cultural or spiritual views, and often reflected English history. Shakespeare drew from ancient history as well, and used themes he knew would be familiar to his audience.

One of the plays Shakespeare first brought to Lord Chamberlain's Men in 1594 was *Titus Andronicus*. *Titus* was a horror play, and Shakespeare's first tragedy. It takes its inspiration from the ancient plays of Ovid, and is widely considered to have been written with George Peele. Drawing from ancient literature and written with the help of another, the play became a fine example of collaboration between writers. Peele and Shakespeare worked together to please specific audience interests of the time. Peele, who died in 1596, was particularly known for writing rather bloody plays. The gore and carnage present in *Titus* bear his mark. The sheer volume of amputations, rapes, murders and revenge plots alone drew crowds by the score. A central character in the play, Lavinia, presented a fascinating challenge for a seasoned actor. She appears without a tongue, having had it and her hands removed. Her uncle desires to know what happened to her. It would have taken an actor of great skill to perform Lavinia's attempts at communication on stage.

And since this play was performed before the Globe was built, the company had the added challenge of working in different locations.

The Comedy of Errors was performed during the Christmas season at Gray's Inn in 1594. Gray's Inn was not a traditional tavern. It was a complex building called an Inn of Court. An Inn of Court was a bit like a gentleman's club, or a place where professionals gathered in Elizabethan England. It is another example of Lord Chamberlain's Men performing whenever and wherever they could. Incidents of the plague became fewer, and some of the theatres had reopened, but the company was still on the road. This particular performance was so popular that the Inn became literally stuffed with people. It was so crowded that the actors themselves jostled with the audience at the start of the show. Only after the audience was thinned a bit could the performance continue. It is no surprise that this sort of play was very popular with the Londoners of Elizabeth's England. It was written with great skill in the mode of error plays, which used deceptive plot devices to propel the story along. Shakespeare used this model for *Comedy*, but increased and intensified the errors, making the plot an intricate puzzle for the audience to solve.

This performance was a prime example of the sort of groundbreaking work of Lord Chamberlain's Men. Using classical error plays as a base, the company began to creatively mix in modern elements of humor. Theatre had become so sophisticated that actors could easily handle the range and extreme of emotions experienced by their characters. To have attended that performance was to be on the forefront of English theatre as a whole. The company continued this tradition of breaking new acting ground, which was later perfected in the Globe.

Before the Globe opened in 1599, Shakespeare wrote several comedies, and began to write his history plays. *The Taming of the Shrew* can be dated to this time, as well as some of the first of Shakespeare's history plays. Many of them revolved around the English kings, Richard I and Henry IV. *The Taming of the Shrew* is particularly notable here, as it is a good example of the type of comedy that could be seen in English theatres of the time.

The plot is based around the taming of a wild and willful woman named Katherina. Such plots abounded in folklore and it was a story that would have been familiar to any audience. It had wide appeal, and Lord Chamberlain's Men could have performed the play anywhere. The taming of Katherina, which is rather comic, is described with an elaborate metaphor. Shakespeare likened it to training a hawk: something both dangerous and exceedingly difficult to do. This popular sport reference would have resonated with the audience, and the performance was a success. It was the genius of Shakespeare and Lord Chamberlain's Men to reduce the illustration of a play's theme to such simple terms, and they did so with eloquence and skill.

Lord Chamberlain's Men also presented *Love's Labour's Lost*, a courtly play, for Queen Elizabeth during the Christmas season of 1597. It was popular enough to do repeat performances later, when the Globe opened. The play itself was a complicated piece, and may have been as difficult to understand then by a common audience as it is to understand now. The characters' lines often rang with political overtones that even dared to reference existing nobles. In caution, however, the names of these nobles had been changed. It was a very highbrow piece of writing, and the jokes were both subtle and intellectual. Filled with witty lines and sly sexual references, the audience would have realized that the play was a spoof on their own activities in the royal courts. This type of production, acted before the Queen, would have displayed the depth of Shakespeare's writing and the ability of Lord Chamberlain's Men to rapidly switch between low and lofty humor. It was enjoyed by all, and the Queen herself was said to have remarked how much she liked it.

Shakespeare continued to display the breadth of his writing with *A Midsummer Night's Dream.* Written in 1595, it was probably crafted for a wedding, although it was also performed at the Globe for a general audience. The actors were forced to stretch their abilities with *Dream*, as it contained multiple dialects. Shakespeare went even further than that and gave the fairies in the play their own language. Certain core actors in the company, like Richard Burbage, were forced to employ every skill in acting they possessed to pull these roles off convincingly. The theme of this play also veered into perilous territory.

Dream was dangerously sexual in its overtones. Set on Midsummer Eve, it would have evoked memories of old customs in the audience. Midsummer Eve was a traditional holiday in pagan times. Young people slipped away into the woods to pair up and spend the night in romance. The play itself strove to see love as more than physical, and though the characters in the play spoke of such behavior in disapproving tones, the reminder of it would have struck a dark chord with the Puritans of the time. The actors of Lord Chamberlain's Men were testing the boundaries of what they could perform.

When the Globe finally opened, there was much for the Puritans to find fault with in the performances staged there. *Hamlet* hit the stage around 1600, and it rapidly became one of Shakespeare's most popular plays. The Bard had, by this time, perfected his craft and included in the play every element of theatre that drew a large audience. Hamlet was dark and broody, and given to long soliloquies. No doubt these were performed with great precision by Richard Burbage. Shakespeare is certain to have had him in mind when he wrote the part. Burbage was one of the few actors who could accurately memorize such a long part. Though the play was a tragedy, it also contained humorous elements, and overtones of perverse sexuality. It was an opus designed to draw a great crowd, and draw them it did. To seal the play's popularity, it ended with an Elizabethan jig.

The later history plays of Shakespeare probably debuted around the same time as *Hamlet*. Their dramatic content covered a period of history from 1399 to 1547. This included all of Elizabeth's ancestors up to and including her father, Henry VIII. The audience was already familiar with the first *Henry* plays, and historians believe *Henry V* was an inaugural play for the Globe in 1599. Lord Chamberlain's Men used the performance to celebrate the opening of their new stage home. The script mentioned the theatre itself, and even referenced its round shape. Strangely enough, the play did not include the role of the comedic character Falstaff, often portrayed by William Kempe, from the earlier *Henry* plays. The Queen was said to be very fond of the Falstaff role, and audiences certainly were. His removal from this particular piece is still a mystery.

The history plays were very important to the Globe. They satisfied the nobility's need to be recognized as important in English history, and they served as a touchstone for English pride. Any audience could relate to the history plays as, in a very real way, they were the history of the audience itself. The performance of one of these plays, *Henry VIII*, became the most famous performance of Lord Chamberlain's Men in the Globe. This showing became famous not because of the material of the play, but because the show itself ended in catastrophe.

The Globe was a building constructed primarily of wood and had a thatched roof. The inside structures were also made of wood. Building regulations and inspections did not exist during this time in English history. If a structure was needed, and could be built, it was. There was very little thought given to safety concerns, or planning in the case of an emergency. The Globe was a fire hazard from its very conception.

By the time James I became king in 1603, theatre performances had become very complicated. Actors had elaborate costumes, the stage dressing was very involved, and special effects became the hallmark of any good theatre. The performance of *Henry VIII* in 1613 was no different, and it was decided that live canons should be fired to add to the performance. The cannons had been used before, and they always delighted the audience. This time, however, the special effect went terribly awry.

The cannons were located near the roof of the theatre, and the dry thatch. The cannons were often plugged, as well, to keep dust and debris out of the barrel of the cannon itself. To increase the dramatic effect as the actor playing Henry VIII appeared on stage, the cannons were fired. One of the plugs caught fire and fell to the ground. The roof of the Globe was ablaze in almost no time. As smoke from the fire drifted down to the audience, very few people paid any initial attention to it. The audience considered the smoke to be nothing more than a by-product of the initial cannon explosion.

The timbers of the theatre caught fire very quickly and the audience roared to life as they finally realized what had happened. A stampede of people fled the building as it burned to the ground. The whole incident took very little time and in less than two hours, the Globe was no more. The eyewitness accounts of the theatre fire were documented. These same documents recorded that no one was seriously harmed. In the ensuing chaos of the Globe's destruction, only one injury was reported. A man's trousers caught fire as he ran away to safety. He suffered only minor injuries, though, before someone snuffed the flames with a bottle of ale. It was considered a miracle that no one had died.

Although the Globe had burned to the ground, there was no loss of life. Lord Chamberlain's Men suffered no lasting consequences from the incident. The Globe was rebuilt the following year, in 1614. By then, many of the original Chamberlain's Men had retired or died. The great Bard himself was gone in 1616. The Globe would take on new actors, but it would never again mirror the magic of that original cast of characters. Shakespeare's plays continued to grace the stage. His fame remained undiminished, and it provided the Globe many more years of success, before it finally closed for good in 1642.

Chapter 5: The King's Men and the End of Elizabethan Theatre

King James I ascended the throne of England in 1603. Since Lord Chamberlain's Men were the most celebrated acting company in London, the new king naturally took them as his personal players. They were renamed the King's Men to reflect their royal patronage. Though they were supported by the previous queen, and often performed for her, the company now had royal patronage in an official capacity. They were given a new charter, new permissions to perform in the Globe, and were even given costumes and cloth to perform in the king's coronation celebration. King James I was an educated man, and supported many types of art. The King's Men performed for him numerous times through the years 1603 to 1608. He was a fan of the theatre, but his interest was much more academic than that of the late queen. He was said to be very religious as well, and his ascension brought with it greater overtones of moral judgment. The Globe had entered a new era.

The plague disrupted the theatres again in 1609 and the company was forced to travel. They performed at court, but were more often found touring the country. Their notoriety never diminished and they added new actors in 1610. Both John Underwood and William Ostler entered the King's Men with established careers. Ostler was considered to be a great actor, and married the daughter of original Globe sharer, John Heminges, in 1611. When Ostler died suddenly in 1614 without a will, his shares of the Globe were seized by his father-in-law, Heminges. Heminges was later sued by his own daughter for control of the assets, though she failed to wrest them from her father. It was this incident that was often used to paint Heminges as a shrewd miser. John Underwood first became famous as a boy actor. He starred in many of Ben Jonson's plays, and was a favorite with the audience. He was soon included among the sharers of the King's Men, and boasted shares of both the Globe and the Blackfriars Theatres.

When James I died in 1625, his son Charles I took the throne. Charles had his own acting troupe, Prince Charles' Men, and the actors of the Globe were concerned that they would no longer have royal patronage. Their concerns were short lived, however, as Prince Charles Men dissolved quickly after their patron's ascension to the throne. They could not compete with the fame the King's Men wielded, and they had lost their lead actor years before. Eliard Swanston had already left Prince Charles Men in 1622 and brought his prestige to the troupe at the Globe in 1624. Shortly after, the King's Men were again awarded a royal charter. Though history records him as a famous player, Swanston carried the more dubious distinction of having presided over the end of the King's Men.

In 1642, civil war threatened England. The Puritan parliament fought the nobility for control of the country. That same year, the parliament took control of London and ordered all of theatres closed. The players of the King's Men tried to keep the troupe together for several years in the chaos that followed, but were largely unsuccessful. There was a period of leniency in 1647, during which the theatres reopened. The King's Men tried to recapture the audiences of London, but they had lost many of their greatest actors by then. Swanston himself left in 1642 and became a jeweler, as well as a puritanical Presbyterian convert. The leniency did not last long. Members of the company were arrested two different times for lewd behavior while in the midst of a performance, in 1648, and again in 1649. The Puritans had finally won.

When the Puritanical oppression later eased, and the theatres opened again in 1660, the era of the Elizabethan play house was over. The companies had scattered to the winds, and many of the old theatres had been demolished, including the Globe. The open-air structures had been replaced with modern versions. Dark enclosed buildings became the normal venue for theatres in England. Tickets for these new theatres were high priced and the theatres were built specifically for the elite. They no longer catered to or cared for the interests of the common people. The old playwrights were also gone. And although Elizabethan plays were still performed, they had been rewritten to reflect newer tastes. The dramas of the French king, Louis XIV, dictated theatre fashion for England.

Chapter 6: The Legacy and Legend

It is uncertain whether the actors and playwrights in Elizabeth's England guessed at how much they would influence world history. Most of them came from humble origins, and probably desired nothing more in the beginning than to make a good living. They followed their gifts, as crafters of written drama, or as entertainers. Above all, the writers and actors of Lord Chamberlain's Men filled a specific need at a specific time. There will always be a crowd ready to be dazzled by a talented group's ability to tell a good story. Lord Chamberlain's Men were masters at supplying this demand.

Entertainment, and the pursuit of a comfortable living, is a powerful motivation to innovation. Whether it was a new way of telling a story, or a new building to house those who listened, the cast and crew of Elizabethan theatre strove first to please their audience. Fame and fortune certainly followed. If they were nervous about inventing a whole new kind of theatre, they certainly never let it show; no good stage actor would. They kept the show alive, despite threats from religious leaders, in-fighting between the various actors, changes in venues, or the loss of a financial backer. Even the threat of death from the plague could not dampen the theatre for long.

The legend of the great Elizabethan theatre continues to influence the world today. The mixture of the greatest playwrights in history with enormous innovations in acting served to accelerate a period of theatre evolution that has never been repeated. Shakespeare's language lives on into the modern world. Whether it is television, movies, or video games, the echoes of Shakespeare and his company will likely be heard for generations to come.

Bibliography

Absoluteshakespeare.com. Copyright 2000-

2005. http://www.absoluteshakespeare.com

Adams, Joseph Quincy. *Shakespearean*

Playhouses: A History of English Theatres from

the Beginnings to the Restoration. Houghton

Mifflin Company, 1960.

Bardstage.org. Copyright 2005.

http://www.bardstage.org

Evans, G. Blakemore. *Elizabethan-Jacobean Drama: The Theatre in Its Time*. New Amsterdam Books, 1988.

Hudson, Henry Norman. *Shakespeare: His Life, Art, And Characters, Volume I*. Library of Congress, 1872.

Jenkins, Elizabeth. *Elizabeth the Great*. Coward-McCann Inc., 1958.

Kermode, Frank. *The Age of Shakespeare*. Modern Library Chronicles, 2003.

Sachs, William J. *The Transformation of Anglicanism: From State Church to Global Community*. Cambridge University Press, 1993.

Shakespeare Online. Copyright 2000-2014.

http://www.shakespeare-online.com

TheatreHistory.com. Copyright 2002.

http://theatrehistory.com

Printed in Poland
by Amazon Fulfillment
Poland Sp. z o.o., Wrocław

59007985R00083